Provenance

Dear "mrs." Hardman
(Penny)
you are all in
here.

B. Clark

Provenance

Poems by Liz Chang

Book&Arts Press

2007

Provenance
Poems by Liz Chang

Copyright © 2007 by Liz Chang

All rights reserved.
No part of this book may be
reproduced or transmitted in any form
or by any means, electronic or mechanical,
including photocopying, recording,
or by any information storage and retrieval system,
without permission in writing from the publisher.

Published by

Book&Arts Press
P. O. Box 199
Wynnewood, PA 19096-3810
www.book-arts-press.com

Design by Jon A. Pastor & Liz Chang
Photography by Liz Chang

Library of Congress Control Number: 2007934953

ISBN 978-0-9795861-1-8

1.0.0

*for Katharine, who started all of this
and for Nicole—if you're going back, take me with you*

What real, unpredictable people we have become.

Poems

Acknowledgments

First, I would like to thank those poets and teachers who have taken the time to guide me and who have given me something akin to faith—in myself and in my writing. I cannot begin to describe the contribution of my classmates and friends to this collection. Thank you to those who have always encouraged me in my exploration of identity—even when you couldn't help asking, "Haitian poetry, huh? Is there a lot of money in that?"—among them: the Clan, the New York delegation, everyone from the Slovenia residency , my VC girlies and my Frisbee® boys (you know who you are). I am more myself for having known you.

I am eternally grateful to everyone at Borders Books in Wynnewood. You welcomed me into your family when I needed you the most. I am also indebted to the staff of Book&Arts Press, Meg Kennedy and Jon Pastor, without their constant prodding—and coddling—I would never have come this far. ("There is no amount of glitter…") Finally, I want to thank my family for their unconditional support of my artistic whim, and especially mention my younger sister Dinah, whose *carte orange* photo did not make the book, but who is definitely present in these pages.

Introduction

*"So this place is as lonely as it feels?" I asked her.
"Yes it is lonely. Are you happy here? ... I love it
more than anywhere in the world. As if it were a
person. More than a person."
"But you don't know the world," I teased her.
... "Is the world more beautiful, then?"
And how to answer that? "It's different," I said.*
       – Jean Rhys, Wide Sargasso Sea

Most of my life, I've lived in and around Philadelphia. I tried to leave once already, and have found my way back—always with vague intention of leaving again. This place has a lot to do with who I am, with who I've become, and I am primarily interested in studying identity. My intention has always been to observe how people present themselves. I had hoped to approach Fashion Design as a study of the outward projection of who a person thinks they are, internally. My poetry tends to focus on my identity: as a woman, as a biracial individual whose appearance is often interpreted as subscription to a culture she knows nothing about (and frequently, not even the one from which she has descended), and always as a lover, friend, daughter, sister and American. So many of these pieces are tied to place and time, constantly weaving in, out and back through each other. They were written over a period of four years, in various locations, including: Philadelphia, New York City, Charleston, Los Angeles, Costa Rica, Grenoble, St. Petersburg (Florida), Barcelona, Hawaii, and Slovenia. For that reason, the poems in this collection are not arranged chronologically, but in a conversational manner; if one work spoke to another place or time, in theme or tone, they are grouped together. If I have one wish for the reader, it would be this: Travel. Be. Love.

Water Main

In the light of the moon pulled down,
I saw her insides, mechanical and ordinary.

Nameless workers with their covered heads and hands
reach into the hot-cut hole past

copper pipes blown blue from their body heat.
Tracing the lines, they locate the rupture.

The foreman emerges from the pit,
wiping his nose with the back of a glove.

He speaks with my mother's blood on his septum:
The drains are in. She leaked more than anticipated.

I learn to flush the lines, to push the bilge
along the tube with my fingernail, drawing

fluid under my gentle pressure. She asks me to
and I'm her daughter.

If You Become a Crocus
in a Hidden Garden,
I Will Be a Gardener

after "The Runaway Bunny" by Margaret Wise Brown

You've cried only once, for me.
When I was lap-sized and slippery
you tried to trim my nails,
to scrape out from underneath
my baby fingermoons
the bits of the world
I'd collected in my short travels
through your manicured life.

I see you
grasping each wiggly digit
like a spring sprout
growing too wild.
I imagine I screeched
at your clipping
of my wings.

Then you slipped and snipped
my lavender skin.
You cried out,
suddenly fearful,
knowing it would not
be the last time.

Manhattan Snowstorm

"And the next time we meet is a new kind of hell, oh.
Both our hearts have a secret: we both love the snow."
— Josh Ritter

Coming back, all I see is
the omnipresent trash heap
underneath the fresh cover—
built up each week
and washed away,
a tide removing
an abandoned sand castle.
The pristine cover, surreal,
becomes the unburdened brow
of a giant corpse.

I remember the way
the grey breath of the city
always seeped
into the flakes so quickly
they fell
from the sky
as sludge.
That grey might have felt familiar,
like surrender.

But this snow forces stillness
and I am reconsidering
the city so far removed

from my recast life as she swells
in a silent crescendo until
I see her as she is:
sewn up, satiated, whole,
the shell of an abuser
splayed out on the table
in the morgue.

Like the coroner's sheet,
snow lays down
on our city with finality.
Bleached of her fury,
she deserves my forgiveness.

Appealing to Peonies

In the regimented garden
of my childhood home,
displaced peonies felt
shamed and broken.
Their skeletal stems shivered
under the burden of
their own cloying smell.

The only evidence
of their departed wild spirits
the slow bob
of their heavy heads
smacking against the house
like ghosts.

But when I approached them
and lifted their ancient faces
to the sun, newsprint petals
always told me
of some other time
when they were glorious.

Survivors

*On April 4, 1991, a helicopter and a small private
plane collided over Merion Elementary School at
lunchtime. There were seven casualties. A second-
grader sustained second and third degree burns
over 90% of his body, and lived.*

I watched you as you melted,
animatedly shaking bits
of your own flesh free—
instinctually, like a dog
shakes to dry himself.

You were wet everywhere, slimy
with nylon. You ran towards me,
carrying your own thick smoke
in an ominous cape hung
around your shoulders.
My screams wilted in the heat
and your jacket advanced
inevitable as glaciers
crossing the scarring
regions of your body.
I turned and ran.

(The image of your mother, screaming,
her cries escalating as the grown-ups restrained her,
Where is he? Where is my son? is branded
on my brain and will always be labeled:
ultimate desperation and despair.)

Afterwards, my mother
took me out for ice cream.
I knew it was a special day—
a different day—but all I could do
was stare and stare
as the rainbow sprinkles wept into the milk.

§℞

You say that 'lucky' is winning the lottery
not living on after you should have died.
You didn't choose this, this luck found you
in the form of a pilot's cockiness and
a crackling, metal rain that fell like the apocalypse
on this small town. But there is no bitterness in your voice.

The only time I see you crack is
when we go out to a diner for sundaes
and the waitress raspily inquires
(in a voice fortified by cigarette smoke),
What happened to *him*?
like you have a disease that she hopes
isn't transferable via tip.

You never confront them,
never level your glassy eyes
at them, their bruised blue of a tsunami
swelling beneath a bottomless boat.

You smolder silently, finish your Hot Fudge,
and decline to go back.

I want to stand up, want to scream:
He didn't do anything to deserve this!
His sin was going to school when he was seven!
We are the ones that look away!
We are the ones that might have protected him!

But I don't. My silence then and now
scorches my throat leaving behind
blackened footprints that won't be replaced
as easily as the ones outside our classroom.
This is how we've come through
the last sixteen years:
changed and still burning.

Truth as Told by the Sexes

from Portrait of a Rattlesnake Skinner,
Sweetwater, TX, by Richard Avedon

In the language of the transgender community, ze
is a gender-neutral pronoun and hir (pronounced "here")
can be used as the plural or possessive pronoun.

Hir look is confrontation
or presentation.
Ze stands stiffly still
straining with the
decapitated
snake clutched,
displayed before hir.
Hir arms buckle
under the weight of
the new carcass.
                         Her
threat removed.
She flops quietly.

Pensive, aggressive,
honest and unfazed
ze wears an apron
spattered with blood
and inattention.
("Let them see what they've done,"
she said in her grief.)
Donning reptilian innards

delicate and cold,
misshapen pink pearls
clack against each other
along a thin intestine-chain,
grasped in a gloved hand
of lacy, fatty flesh.

Ze stares past the lens,
with the defiant pride
of a toddler: Look
at what I've done.
Hir eyes reflect the cold light
of testimony. This is what I do.
I carve out
what makes her *her*.
I romance them.

On Dreaming of My Wedding Day

I saw him again
as he is (because that's how
I need him to be): a crumpled,
white, flat vision—
the way I've dragged him
out of the trash
so many times.

It was a perfect day,
(that day in the diner, under
the unforgiving orange lights)
a day I knew I'd waited for
(I knew I'd lost him,
knew he'd first let go of who I was)
and he floated towards me,
in cheap, rumpled linen.

His face was empty,
inescapable. (I pulled myself
through the air,
breaststroking past waves of doubt)
He reached for me,
and for a second, I saw him
as he used to be:
with his boyish hair
and smile.
And even in my sleep,
I said no.

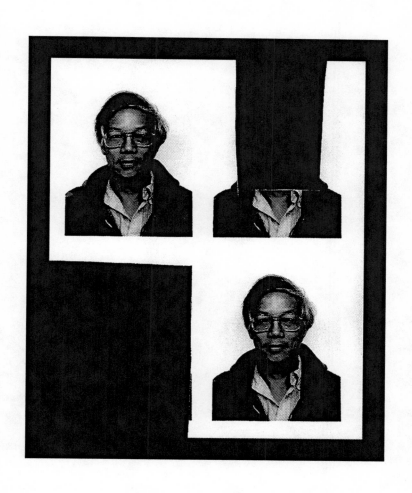

Citrus Odes

"The window opens like an orange
Lovely fruit of light."
          – Guillaume Apollinaire

FOR MGC

Despite dinner, the appearance
of an orange at the table afterwards
meant a temporary stay-of-execution.

I'd watch my father's measured
wrist movements, his pocket knife
circumscribing the northern third,
incising and discarding the lid.
He'd cut the rest into quarters,
mapping it confidently,
section by section
the familiar globe.

My lesson lay in
the precision of that deconstruction:
a study in juiceless efficiency.
I remember
the soft rip of the peel
as it released the white flesh:
like the sound of wet plaster spreading,
sealing over the soft spots in our relationship.

After bearing witness,
I am reinitiated each time
as a silent participant
with segments carefully untangled
from their cobwebbed crypts
and offered up like an apology.

FOR MDF

Undressing an orange
is something I get my fingers into.
There's no conservation.
I aim to chisel through its layers, peeling away
old skins revealing dry wall,
then sheetrock, down to the studs—the skeleton.
And I'll knock that down too,
swinging my sledgehammer-shoulders.

If the juice rests in the alleys of my fingernails,
stinging slightly, so much better.
You taught me to love a little pain,
to thank the man who twists my arm
demonstrating how to escape even
dislocation shooting through me in biting waves.

I needed the little bit of abandon
you brought. The moments of calm,

when you took off your armor,
I knew I'd need to preserve
inside myself, a monument
of peel-scales, so I stacked the orange innards
and tried to build myself a shelter
against the pain of your departure.

(It knocked me out anyway.)
I'd smile and breathe in Orange Pekoe,
sweetened by the aftertaste of adrenaline.
I thought it would become my methadone.
But without my brother, there is no transcendence,
just dark water, with the far-off smell
of the citrus-tinged oxygen that used to sustain me.

I tear myself up, remembering my resolve
to be the sister he would adore. It was always too late.

FOR MDK

I tear out the delicate core at the belly
of the orange, and think of the moment
I exposed myself to you:
ripping raw truth out from
a deep grave inside my intestines,
and feeling it catch
as I extract it through my navel.

You caress my stem, considering it. Gently,
you deny my violence, unzip
my mandarin-colored dress and
push open my legs.

Individually-packed pockets
of self-control explode in my ears.
I breathe in bursts, trying
to devour you.
I feel the insides of
my eyelids, suddenly.
I delve into every pore, exploring
the regular texture,
as they curl upwards, drying.

I press my tongue against
the secret overlap of
my bottom-front teeth
and you fall against me again
as I imagine
sucking out small tears
from freed citrus segments
gently peeling them from
their vein-crossed base.

You stop to ask me what I want.
All at once, I wish

to treat you like an orange:
enjoying every inch of you,
playfully rolling bits
of membrane between my fingers,
leaving shallow prints
that disappear slowly, erasing my presence.

As a Lightbulb

I want to feel cast
of one shape,
brittle like a shell,
the brush of your
frayed nail-edge sending
delicate shudders through me.

I want to know
every inch of
my curves, to feel
smooth and complete.
I am so many surfaces
sometimes
and you, with your cradling hands,
you find edges
I can't feel
from the inside.

I want to feel radiant,
in control of
the tiny purpose
inside of me
that warms us both
and pulses against
my limits. I want to
push my capacity
to open to light.

On January 2, 2007, Wesley Autrey *"dived onto the tracks of a southbound No. 1 train in Manhattan... to save another man's life. ...[H]is two daughters... [ages 4 & 6] watched as he dived to the trackbed."*
                                                                —New York Times *4 Jan 2007*

Underground: Two Fictions

1

She wakes on her back, the edge of
his solid ribcage pressing her flat
against the roach casques and rails,
in the breath before the train meets them.
The thrash of the express drags their tangled bodies under,
beneath the frozen depths of inundation
of eight million strangers constantly banging against her guard, and
she feels his heavy, clotting cologne and harsh cheek
over her, feels the restraint of his legs against her,
stubbornly crushing her, trying to mold her to him, replace her.
For five metallic seconds, she lets him.
Her lungs seize and inside that white clarity,
she thinks of him on the platform:
shifting his weight, bobbing his head to remembered drums.
(Outside the station, by the downtown entrance every day.)
She suddenly loves him and it is terrible.
The last car flows around the corner,
southbound. He dismounts, and doesn't try to speak.

2

I wanted to go to the zoo
to see the seals. 'Watch them sleep and
dive off the rocks into the green pool.
My Daddy says we'll take Tallulah too.
I wear my pink raincoat on my head
because it's still cold, but did you know
the seals live there all year round,
even when we don't see them?

I dangle my arms, swing back and forth
with my Daddy, and we sing and dance along
to the pickle-drums they play there
everyday, on our way down
into the subway. He says I dance like a wild animal
and maybe I belong in the zoo,
and I say, No, Daddy! I belong with you!

He laughs and I hold onto his sanded hand—
its newspapery smoothness—and think of the seals.
Drying in the ashen noon on the rocks,
they look like the teenagers that hang on our stoop.
Out of water, their hides grow cracks
so big a grown-up could fall down into them.

I hold onto his hand and don't see the man fall
until Daddy throws me down and at first I think
Tallulah pushed me and I jump up to push her back but

I see her braids flopping in her big dark eyes—
I know she's afraid. Where is my Daddy?
The train flashes past like the angriest storm:
all thunder and lightning, and I hold onto my sister,
because I know how she hates the noise.

Nature Morte: Still Life

I was driving
reminding myself
that this pain
and the green
that shades this street
is still life without you
and I lost myself in
a Dalí dreamscape.
It felt dangerous,
the foliage lying down
or sharpening, so I'd see
the details of their
stems growing like explosions
with the grimace
of all that noise
on the face
of every leaf.
I was outside your house.
And lying sideways in the street,
a moment of respite,
was a flapping ear.
The fly-flicking edge
dancing wildly in the wind.
The ear grew to a head:
with an ebony snout,
still wet with quenched breath
and two dark, glassy eye-fruits

beneath sculpted horns.
A trophy of natural
accomplishment,
discarded in the street.
I noticed someone
had cleaned up the carnage:
No mayonnaise spill of marrow,
or strawberry-stains of blood
smeared on the asphalt.
No leftover fragments of bone
and carcass masquerading
as branches or leaves.
No tracks left, at all.

Encounter at the Mütter Museum

*For Kim Sun-Il, a Korean translator stationed in Iraq
who was beheaded by Al-Qaeda; the tape of his death
was distributed to television stations worldwide.*

They passed around the magnetic reel
of his death like pornography.
It is a time-weary dance: machete meets neck,
falls in love with neck, falls.
His death felt as inconsequential as romance.
In the dark theatre of the BBC,
we were all alone, masturbating
to what we shouldn't watch.

But even in low-resolution, his features
were emotionless and dark,
and I saw every boy I've ever known.
A child kneeling before his captors,
his face composed, rubbed over
with the patina of something beyond terror.
Like looking through glass into inevitability.

So when I met the shrunken head
it surprised me with its calm
taut grey skin pulled over petrified cheekbones
lashstems like freckles along the ridge
of closed eyes, swollen lips resting

agape, no trace of the horror
of having been severed, the shame and injustice
drained away in years beneath the sand.

God, may he forgive us.

Infinite Elizabeth

I imagine she dyed her hair
at this age as a marker:
the way scientists tag the wing
of a captured specimen—for future study.

I watch her memorize the pattern of
leopard spots on her signature tissues
when she thinks no one is looking.

I feel her steel herself against
that day when she will have to set down
for good, the light gone from her eyes.

She will still be able to narrate
her many photographs, her reincarnations
saying, See the wild one
with the purple hair? That's me.

Rambla dels Ocells
Barcelona, 2004

"La Rambla dels Ocells *(Avenue of the Birds) contains
a bird market...[with] a line of cages on either side
of the street."*   – The Rough Guide to Barcelona

At night the stands are monuments
to local shows and anarchy
but through the plastic walls and locks
I hear them beg to be fed.
In the frosted dark
their calls expire instantly.

> After dinner and sangria,
> I wish I were a bird stand
> with my fluttering desires neatly caged
> and securely bolted inside.
> But my secret residents flap nervously
> just below my skin.

In the soft, grey day
they are wrestled away
from their safety and put on display:
fantastic wares
whose fate may be love
or the diningroom table.

I marvel at roosters wearing spats,
like honored guests at a dinner party.
And lovebirds shifting

fickly from pair to pair.
I justify their need for body heat.

> Stubborn, insistent
> the burgeoning crescendo of the
> residents' activities fill my ears,
> drowning out the part of me that
> whispers to the frantic aviary:
> *You haven't chosen this closed life yet,*
> *You still have a chance.*

The city pigeons hover nearby.
I hear them squawking,
"Let my people go!"
hurling themselves uselessly
at the cages in public protest.
But soon I realize that they're
whoring themselves for food
discarded on the ground
as the attendant sloshes the meal
on the sidewalk.

> This world has been unlocked for me,
> and I wonder if one day
> I couldn't shiver and choke,
> bursting open, belching birds, fears and
> confessions like a feathery
> Pandora's box.
>
> Would it be so bad to live exposed?

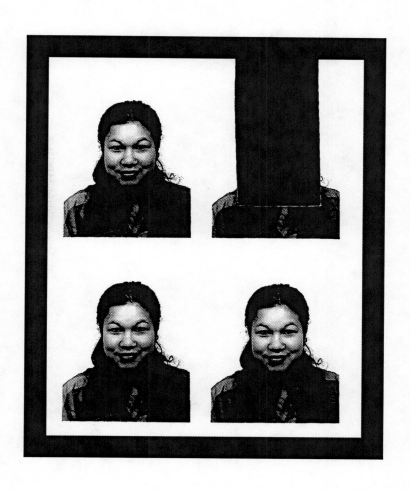

Déluge

*"She is in love with the beautiful formlessness
of the sea."*   – *Sylvia Plath*

I learned from him to love
the sea before I knew the danger
of its inconstancy. It was
the power that drew us
to the shore, reclaiming
something vast and wild
that had drained from our lives.

We sat in silence
his shoulder rested against mine.
In the whipping air,
tiny bits of sediment
stuck to every unprotected inch.
When he shifted, a salty
silhouette clung to my skin.
I loved watching him gather and crash.

But the greatest lesson was the tide
casting itself at the mercy of the shore.
With each incremental death,
the offspring it carries slipped gracefully
into tiny strawholes in the sand.
Bruised shells clasped closed
fading away like bells, chiming:

Love will ask terrible things
and your best answer
will be silence.

Jellyfish:
Traveling Exhibit/Limited Engagement

It seemed important
to take the picture
of you
your watch
your grown-up watch
resting against the tank
of ethereal jellyfish.

They float, propelled
by some invisible wave
suspended in a mass of
their own detritus.
In the blacklight,
the shit has more presence.

They don't know time,
or understand my urgency.
Time for us is inextricable
from hunger and death.
They wound with a lightning storm
of pain and there is
no sacrifice in that.
They incapacitate, and digest slowly.

I knew hunger so amorphous,
pulsing-real and menacing,

it attacked over and over:
a constant death.

At the bottom of that emptiness
(in the end, there is an end)
it's only a matter of time.
In that instant—*snap*—
it's all over.

Mermaid Story

All weekend, I've been
knocked   about
by the tide
between us.

I fight the pull of you,
                         knowing it is not me that churns you up.

But I am discovering the sea,
        and ignoring
the plastic sentinels
        that define the safe realm of our friendship
        (bobbing, the line blurs forgivingly),
I wade into your bedsheets,   my feet sinking slightly.

I thought your body
would be like driftwood:
        barely substantial, lighter
than its look, battered.
                But you are here, against me,
                cresting with the solid
                stubbornness of a wave
                drawing in and out.

(I feel it: *her*   pulsing beneath   the water as an undercurrent.)

I wallow in the salty shock of your tongue
                and the familiar depth   of your breath
                                        inside my mouth.

I dive under, wanting so badly
                    to belong to this new world.

"You taste like Yuengling,"
I whisper, hoping to draw you back,
knowing you'll hear what I mean: *you taste like home.*

You speak into the wind,
                    and I lean in
                              to listen to
          the curved shell of your lips:
                              "You don't taste
                              like anything."

(Yuengling is a brewery based in Western Pennsylvania)

50

Profile

for J.

The line of his chin frightens me,
because it is the only honest thing about him.
Handsome and hostile, the skin clings
to the bone like a tailored jacket
floating around a torso, with just the right amount
of breathing room: just so
a voice raised in anger won't burst the stitches.
They yawn to accommodate.
I remind myself that each small head
that's rested underneath his chin
has left a groove, like the sigh of stone stairs
in a tourist destination. From inside that cradle,
I hear him chewing on his loss,
and he confesses how the first time
the carpet left its lunar impression on his cheek.
Oh, god, oh god! I've peed in her!
He says he thought,
not yet knowing how to draw back,
to inflate the space between him and the lover
amidst his shuddering. Sixteen years
into this dance, he uses the careful cover of those seconds
now, knowing that invulnerability
will be read as embarrassment.
He counts on it.
He's been caught off-guard only once,

when that first one called, saying she had to talk to him
about What Happened. He panicked and took the car out.
Drove away, but came back, his parents pulled in
just as he turned the lights off. Told them
he was just checking them, and stepping in
out of the yellow hiss of the floods,
Jim cold-cocked him right in the jaw.
His mother, that angel warrior, didn't lift
her hand to stop it.
I feel his cheek click and lock
even now and I think of the moments of silence
before a movie, when the screen darkens.
(I'm close enough—I should see my face
on the blank screen of your eyes.
They've been wiped clean
and the moments spin away.)
Clicking down to the performance:
5... 4... 3... 2...

Outside the Muzej Talcev OR
Inside the Katzenstein Psychiatric Hospital

This site, a former mansion in Begunje, Slovenia, was appropriated during World War II by the Nazis for use as a gestapo prison. Portions of the cellblocks are preserved and open to tour groups, while the rest of the grounds are occupied by a state-run psychiatric hospital.

A woman stands at the second-story
window, smoking, in her bathrobe.
She lifts the cigarette to her stained lips
then drops her hand disdainfully.
She reaches to smooth the hair
against the cold clamshell of her cheek,
watching the tourists below, watching her,
because she knows that's what they expect.
She lifts the cigarette to her stained lips and
shifts her weight, as she has just seen
the woman outside do, who stands
by the path smoking, sucking in her pink freedom.

Behind the sill, the woman inside stands
awkwardly, her legs apart, feet flat,
underwear pulled too high and tight
against her stomach by the orderly.
She wastes no movement on herself.
This life is a constant cover and never so real
as when she is breathing in the wet pillowcase,
savagely clawing at her own neck, trying to dislodge

the pinecone of another year inside this hell caught
in her throat. Time flows out of her despite the tourniquet
as she relives every despairing instant of her 12,000 lives
happening now, always, in this prison, in the present.

Someone pulls the pillowcase tighter and deep inside her
something lurches as she tries to scream,
and finds she has no voice. The woman outside,
hearing this, looks up.

for Sarah

Checking In

You are really sitting here,
in this crackly green chair
shifting with the Ladies near you.
He's really out there—six hours.
Watching bad television that warns against
what happens When Parents Dress Too Sexy,
doing homework, next to his mother.

You will be called by name,
and you will feel it fall away
as they show you where the pre-op room door
leads into the other room
without the safety of a hallway.

Here's
       where to leave your clothes. Shed them.
       Where to find the telling gown. Unwrap it.
       Where to sit/shiver in the chairless corner
       until they call you again.

Then you will lie back and talk about your future
even when you feel you'll rip in half
from the pushing-prodding alien supports
that force you open far enough so
the Doctor can see what the problem is.

You will hold onto a hand
tight, like your mother's,

were she here (if she knew you were here).
It's Ruthie's only job—
to hold your hand—
although she's dressed like one of them.

Where is your safe neighborhood now?
The lock on your door? The bleached sheets on your bed?
You rest upright and watch the other Ladies'
heads loll from the general anesthesia.
If you're lucky you'll ask for a local,
then you can be there.
See the exam lights, so loud and
hear that voice, from the waiting room,
and feel *what's real* as it melts away.
You'll live to write about it.

On What It's Like to Doubt

I chew doubt
running my tongue along
its thick bark inside my cheek

it cements my flesh
to the porcelain surface of teeth
until breaking away becomes
a juicy crack that happens
all at once with the recoil of a handgun.

Doubt sits on my tongue
and sizzles until all the buds
are blackened in the dry heat.

I breathe in but it begins snapping
against the ribs of the roof and
each pop is the tiny caress
of a stubborn mosquito
indulging in the same flesh
over and over.

A Nose as Private and Public Experience

i.

I catch him pulling his nose shut sometimes,
slowly releasing, child-like in his delight.
The smell inside, he says, is metallic.

He shows off how it's lop-sided.
One nostril pinched shut, lame.
A battle scar from a traumatic game
            of soccer.

He can blow music through his futile one.
Sometimes, when we lie in bed
he serenades me.

ii.

On the street,
I see them watching my nose—
it rises off the flat plane of my face
like a burial mound, distinct and private.

It starts conversations.
"Where…are you…from?" I get
from cab drivers, sandwich-vendors.

I could prattle on about citizenship
and interracial marriages until they
relegate me to the 'miscellaneous' column.

But I know better; after all, they just want
to claim to understand, they just want me
to reflect their own stories of displacement.
So I smile, and turn my silent nose down.

About the Author

LIZ CHANG has lived in and around Philadelphia for most of her life. She has studied in Costa Rica, France and Slovenia. She graduated from Parsons School of Design (a division of New School University) in New York City with a Bachelor's of Fine Arts degree. She is currently enrolled in the Master's of Fine Arts program in Writing through Vermont College. She plans to graduate in January of 2009 with a certificate in translation.

Colophon

The body of *Provenance* is set in several styles and weights of Adobe Minion, created by master calligrapher and type designer Robert Slimbach. Released in several versions between 1990 and 2000, Minion is inspired by classical, old style typefaces of the late Renaissance, a period of elegant, beautiful, and highly readable type designs. Crisp and open, it politely defers to the text, and allows itself to serve as a vehicle without adding its own statement.

Titles and headings are set in Agfa Rotis Semi Serif, a unique hybrid with characteristics of both serif and sans-serif faces. It is one member of a family of four fonts designed by Otl Aicher, and named after the village in the Allgäu where he has lived since 1972. Its quirky combination of formality and informality, stately seriousness and pure fun, brought it to mind for this volume of poetry.

The Book&Arts Press logo is set in Linotype Zapfino, a tour-de-force of type design, a truly calligraphic face with a vast number of variants for most characters, including decorative ("swash") characters like the ampersand ('&') in our logo. Its creator, Hermann Zapf, is universally regarded as one of the greatest calligraphers and type designers of all time. Zapfino has the unique ability to function with equal facility in the most formal *and* the most informal settings.

Printed in the United States
91039LV00002B/1-96/A